This book belongs to

_____

Mother Teresa

By Mary Nhin

This book is dedicated to my children - Mikey, Kobe, and Jojo.

Copyright © 2023 by Grow Grit Press LLC. All rights reserved. No part of this book may be reproduced in any form without permission in writing from the publisher. Please send bulk order requests to growgritpress@gmail.com Printed and bound in the USA. MiniMovers.tv
Paperback ISBN: 978-1-63731-655-9 Hardcover ISBN: 978-1-63731-657-3

Hi, I'm Mary Teresa Bojaxhiu,
but people call me Mother Teresa.

From a young age, I became fascinated by stories of the lives of missionaries who volunteered their time to help the disadvantaged.

I can't explain it, but I felt a strong desire to become a nun and serve the poor.

I traveled to India where I began work as a teacher. While there, I experienced the widespread poverty people were undergoing. I witnessed the Bengal famine of 1943 and the Hindu/Muslim violence in 1946.

These two events made such a deep impression on me that in 1950, I founded the Missionaries of Charity.

My primary mission was to look after...

the hungry, the naked, the homeless, the crippled, the blind, the lepers, all those people who feel unwanted, unloved, uncared for throughout society, people that have become a burden to the society and are shunned by everyone.

We did not have much to give,
but we gave all that we had.

It is not how much we do,
but how much love we put into doing.
It is not how much we give,
but how much love we put in the giving.

In 1952, I opened my first home for the dying, which allowed people to die with dignity. I often spent time with those who were dying. I wanted them to die knowing that someone cared.

Slowly, my work spread around the world.

By 2013, there were 700 missions operating in over 130 countries. The scope of the work of Missionaries of Charity expanded to include orphanages and hospices for those with terminal illnesses.

In 1979, I was awarded the Nobel Peace Prize.

Not all of us can do great things. But we can do small things with great love.

Timeline

1929 – Mother Teresa travels to India

1950 – Mother Teresa starts Missionaries of Charity

1952 – Mother Teresa opens first hospice

1979 – Mother Teresa is awarded Nobel Peace Prize

minimovers.tv

 @marynhin   @officialninjalifehacks
#minimoversandshakers

 Ninja Life Hacks

 Mary Nhin   Ninja Life Hacks

 @officialninjalifehacks

www.ingramcontent.com/pod-product-compliance
Lightning Source LLC
Chambersburg PA
CBHW041524070526
44585CB00002B/78